QUANTUM LIVING

A LIFE FULL OF MIRACLES

DUKE TATE

DISCLAIMER

Be aware that certain supplements and detox protocols may cause a severe detox reaction in some individuals. Please proceed with caution when using these substances and protocols.

This book is not intended to be a substitute for professional medical advice and should not be relied on as health or personal advice. Always seek the guidance of your doctor or other qualified health professional with any questions you may have regarding your health or a medical condition.

CONTENTS

1

THE PROBLEM

When I was very ill with Lyme Disease at twenty years of age, I had many vivid dreams, some of which I recount in my other two books in this series. One dream in particular struck a real chord with me. I was standing in a room looking at the bed I was asleep in at the time. The room, a dull color in reality, was bright white in the dream with sunlight streaming in through the windows, which it rarely did. On the bed, there was a cute little baby. To my right, a Sufi dressed in a green robe pointed to the baby and said, "This is what you were, now see what you have become."

At the time I had this dream, I was quite ill with Lyme Disease and still coping with emotional turbulence from my past. The dream served as a mirror to show me how far I had strayed in my life from the innocent child that was sent here from Reality—that perfect place from where we all originate.

Over the years since having that dream, my Sufi Teachers have helped me to deprogram my conditioning, which has been the single most important thing I have done to radically transform my life.

All our desires, wants, what we think about, choose, believe, is all due to the influence of older individuals in our lives when we were younger.

When I was eighteen, I had my first other-worldly experience. I had taken LSD with some friends and we were dancing to hippie music at the lakefront in Madison, Mississippi one chilly evening over Christmas break in high school. It was a crisp, clear night and the black sky was sprinkled with stars. I twirled around and around in a circle for a long time like a whirling Mevlevi dervish. All of a sudden, my spirit left my body and ascended high in the sky over the lake. I was looking down on the whole assembly when an inner awareness told me, "You are with these people right now because you are from this place and grew up with them." And a minute later, I was jolted back into my body. My friend Davis asked me, "Hey man, what happened to you just then? You looked distant for a moment there?" and I told him.

I am now totally against the recreational use of drugs, and believe the whirling of the Mevlevi dervishes to be repetitive as it is used these days. In any case, this experience caused me to question my life, who I was, what I was doing and where I was heading. My whole identity was so caught up in my Southern roots, Mississippi, and who I knew, that it was key for me to break out of that somehow.

Finding a way out of this rabbit hole is a problem only we as individuals can fix. No one else can do it for us. My dear Sufi Teacher Ali Dede stated that this conditioning can be undone by three methods:

1. A technology such as the Sufi Tradition
2. Emotional Freedom Technique (EFT)
3. Constant Positive Affirmations

To number 2, I want to add Dr. Alex Loyd's Healing Codes. Whether you use one or all of these, it has to be an inside job and only *we* can do our own work. Dede gave me a bicycle, *but I had to ride it*.

One of my strengths is that I just don't give up. I have enormous stickability. Growing up, I was completely devoid of this single important trait. I quit everything. I would jump from one team sport to the next. One year it was soccer, the next, English horseback riding, and the following year, bowling. I was alright at everything, but *never excelled* at anything, which is kind of the opposite of the famous Sufi motto: be the best at what you do. Part of that was my lack of stickability. Dr. Greg S. Reid discusses in his book, *Stickability*, that perseverance is the number one trait successful people have in common. For such people, it's never a question of whether they will reach their goal, it's when.

When overcoming Lyme Disease and chronic illness, I basically had no choice but to stick to getting well, even though it took years and years of hard work and study. *What choice did I have?* It was either stick with recovery, or be ill, and I would not allow myself to stay sick. I just couldn't stand the whole notion that I had to be ill endlessly while others got to feel great. Why them and not me?

That stickability, combined with having a brilliant doctor and Sufi mentor in Ali Dede, allowed me to work through enormous amounts of conditioning with EFT and Dr. Alex Loyd's The Healing Codes.

We all have lots of garbage we pick up from our childhood. We store that inside our hearts, and it just so happens to affect every aspect of our lives. Bruce H. Lipton, Stanford University PhD, states in his book *The Biology of Belief* that research now shows that memories are what affect our cells, not our genes as traditionally thought. His research has proven that 95% of all chronic disease is caused by stress. The remaining 5% is genetic, caused by conditioning on the cells from past ancestors. (Bruce Lipton, 2016). The immune system requires a state of peace in the body to function properly. This is such an important point to emphasize. Whether you like it or not, stress can literally cause us to get sick by reducing our immune systems, which can fight infections off.

It is quite interesting because Ali Dede told me that bi-polarity disorder is caused by a lack of love in childhood. In other words, *bad memories* can make a person bi-polar. What we are talking about now are *cellular memories*. Everything that we perceived to be bad or good when it happened to us – largely determined by where, when and how we manifested in this plane – is stored in our hearts and affects all the cells in our bodies either in a good way, if it's a good memory, or a bad way, if there is a lie written on the memory.

Ali Dede said to me once, "Maintain a very high frequency in your heart, dear Duke, and you will always be well."

2

QUANTUM HEALTH

Regarding chronic disease, the source of the problem as Dr. Bruce Lipton writes are lies written on cellular memories stored in the heart due to conditioning. They may lead to physical problems, but the source is traumatic memory causing stress.

Our bodies are all made of energy. *We are energetic beings.*

The Chinese believe that when we develop an illness, there is an energetic blockage along the meridian points in our bodies. Dede says that when a person is 100% well, their energy or qi is centered in the lower *tantien*, translated literally as "elixir of life field". This important energy center in the field of the Chinese practice of Qi-Gong is three finger-lengths below the navel and two finger-widths behind it.

There are several ways to return one's energy to the lower *tantien*, which I will now go over in depth.

The first is the practice of heartbreathing, while feeling or sensing one's feet.

Heartbreathing, developed by the Heartmath Institute in Big Bear Lake, California, which I mention in the first two books in this series,[1] is a form of creative breathing that produces coherent Heart Rate Variability (HRV) levels. To practice heartbreathing, imagine that the breath coming into your body is entering through the heart center, then think about something you are grateful for while breathing this way. You can purchase an emWave device via Heartmath's website to monitor your progress.

Two other tools that remove energy blockages in the body and undo conditioning, which I also mention in my previous two books in this series,[2] is Emotional Freedom Technique (EFT) and Thought Field Therapy (TFT). EFT is an emotional form of acupuncture that involves tapping on the meridian points while repeating certain positive affirmations. TFT, on the other hand, is tapping on specific Chinese meridian points in a certain order without affirmations.

I suffered with erectile dysfunction (ED) for over thirteen years on and off. I finally cured it permanently by removing the energetic blockage causing it through tapping with EFT for four days straight to a video titled "Sex Issues" on Brad Yates's EFT YouTube channel. I had tried absolutely everything to fix it outwardly and nothing but this worked!

The ancient Chinese practice of Qi-Gong, or Chi-Kung, is a series of movements, breathing and exercises that cultivate and harness qi or life energy in the body, and centers the energy in the lower *tantien*. Dede says that just performing the Pa Tuan Chin Qi-Gong movement everyday can gradually help a person achieve and maintain health.

Developed by the twelfth-century Chinese general Yueh Fei and derived from eighteen exercises that the Bodhidharma recommended to Shaolin monks eight centuries prior, Pa Tuan Chin was practiced daily by the general's soldiers to maintain their health and prepare their bodies for difficult martial arts.

Master Lin, a Chinese Qi-Gong master in Minnesota, developed another truly beneficial form of

Qi-Gong called Spring Forest Qi-Gong. The Mayo Clinic has even scientifically proven that his method reduces stress.

Another way to center the energy in the lower *tantien* is through Dr. Alex Loyd's Healing Codes. I personally had an experience with a very persistent and troublesome ail in my brain that may have been a minor blood clot. Although I did have an MRI, a diagnosis was never confirmed by that or any other test.

During that time, I was still maintaining a very high level of physical, emotional, mental and spiritual health after healing myself from Lyme Disease, multiple chemical sensitivity (MCS), medically confirmed eosinophilic esophagitis and erectile dysfunction (ED) – using spiritual energy from Dede, oxygen therapy, high quality nutrition, various nutrients, positive thinking/affirmations and EFT. But now, none of those things were working, and I was truly distraught. I had used EFT probably 400 times for this one issue without much change.

This particular ailment caused a sort of numbness on the left side of my head in the mornings. It was also quite acute after working out intensely with heavy free weights, after running and after drinking alcohol. I literally couldn't drink more than a little booze without waking up with a splitting headache. For the most part, I was able to ignore it and pretend it wasn't there, living a relatively normal life outwardly, even working up to fourteen hours a day sometimes. My cellular health was quite high, but I still had this one ailment... and it drove me crazy.

The only thing that seemed to improve it was to drink coffee in the morning, from which I had previously abstained for many years. Still, I was determined to have uniform perfect health again in every way and not be dependent on coffee to maintain stamina.

First of all, coffee doesn't give energy and *I knew this* because Dede had told me there was no energy in coffee ever. Coffee actually creates stress in the body by triggering the flight or fight mechanism, which in turn causes various stress hormones to be released. These hormones give the illusion of more energy, but what we are really feeling is stress.

I tried all the various nutrients I had researched online for this ail, thinking there must be something that could eliminate the problem. Proceeding on the assumption that it must be some microscopic blood clot the MRI couldn't perceive, I tried oxygen supplements, oxygenated water, a cayenne pepper supplement, Vitamin E, turmeric, all the usual blood-thinner suspects, but not one thing touched it.

Finally, distraught, I wrote to Dede about it and he recommended a truly remarkable therapy called Brainspotting. I immediately found a practitioner in Orlando, Florida, and set up an appointment with her.

Brainspotting was developed by therapist David Grand while using Eye Movement Desensitization and Reprocessing Therapy (EMDR)—a therapy based on the premise that the movement of the eyes can unlock certain traumas stored in the body. One day, while working with EMDR, Grand's client had a cathartic release of emotion when he stopped and focused on one particular point with his eyes. This breakthrough led Grand to develop the therapy known today as Brainspotting.

My first session with the Orlando practitioner went very well. I had good results with my head issue as it significantly reduced the numbness. I used it for a few weeks on my own after returning home. However, I could never totally eliminate the ailment.

So I wrote back to Dede, informing him about my progress, and he suggested I read Dr. Alex

Loyd's book *The Healing Codes*. On the day I received the book, I read the whole thing in one sitting and began to use the codes at once.

Dr. Loyd has a truly remarkable story.

When his wife became clinically depressed with bi-polar disorder shortly after they were wed, he—a minister at the time—searched endlessly for a cure, even praying every day for her for the next twelve years. His wife and he exhausted every treatment they could find, but nothing worked to eliminate her depression.

One day, while flying back home from a quantum physics seminar in Los Angeles, Dr. Loyd was praying for his wife who had experienced a very bad attack of depression and loneliness. All of a sudden, he saw a set of healing codes in his mind's eye to help a person overcome any stress and illness in their life. For the next three hours, he transcribed them on his notepad, and the rest is history.

These "codes" are different combinations of self-administered hand-holds over the face, head and neck area without actually touching the areas, to address different problems and conditions. Before performing the hold, the individual thinks of the traumatic memory, then they rate the discomfort on a scale of 0 to 10—10 being the worst and 0 being no feeling. After that, the individual selects his or her truth statement they feel is best for their issue, and a special prayer provided by Alex is evoked. Then, the first hand position is held. While holding the position, the individual focuses on the truth statement. Then, the subsequent positions are held.

From my use of the very first code, I was hooked.

Over the next few days I began to experience a dramatic improvement in my head and continued using them for many months afterwards. Since then I have gone back to working out with weights and even reached my lifelong goal of doing a full set of 8 reps bench-pressing 225 pounds, being able to skip the coffee and drink alcohol without a headache the next morning.

I still use the codes now, always with amazing results. I have released issues from my childhood in minutes that were affecting every aspect of my life without my knowing it.

I would like to share a few of my experiences using these codes below, as it may help you to understand how they work and operate.

When I was a small child, I was terribly shy with girls my age. One day, I was swimming at wave park called Rapids on the Reservoir in

Ridgeland, Mississippi, when a girl came up and told me her friend liked me. At the time, I was standing at the foot of the wave pool with a soaking wet shirt on. I only swam with shirts on because they protected my pale, freckled skin from the sun. I used to burn terribly. Right after she told me, I turned around and flipped the girl the middle finger. Quite naturally, she got scared and ran off.

I was rejecting myself before she could.

Back then, I was so self-conscious about how I looked, with countless freckles and red hair—so different from many of my friends—that I didn't think anyone could ever like me.

At first, I think I responded as if it was a practical joke, since I was often criticized during recess at the football field by various cute girls in my class. But in my heart, I sensed the girl's message was sincere, and perhaps that was even more painful to face than any rejection she could express. I was rejecting myself before she could.

THE THOUGHT of this memory used to bring tears to my eyes, but since using these Healing Codes, it is nothing. And it is just one of many buried memories from my past that I healed from using this special technology.

I will now share another example with you.

I have loved water since I was a child. My favorite movie has always been *What Lies Beneath* (2000), a haunting ghost story set in Addison, Vermont. I was so infatuated with this movie that I used to want to move to Addison, a small town on Lake Champlain next to Burlington, Vermont's capital city. I took countless trips there to visit friends and always loved it.

Spoiler alert! In it, Harrison Ford's character, a professor, has an affair with a student, and when she threatens to tell his wife, he murders her and throws her body in the lake behind his house. His wife, played by Michelle Pfeiffer, starts being visited by the ghost of the girl. She repeatedly tells Ford's character of these visits and he finally drugs her so she cannot move, and places her in the bathtub on a paralyzing agent in order to drown her.

Once I started working with The Healing Codes, my obsession with the movie became obvious. An acquaintance of mine had tried to drown me at our neighborhood swimming pool when I was younger. We were just horsing around, but it went on way too long and felt too real, and I couldn't breathe. I wanted to punch him in the groin, but I knew that would only provoke him further, and I thought he might actually not let me go. When I finally came up, I was truly scared and gasping for air.

What is so ironic is that I was always so thirsty for water growing up. I drank so much more water than most kids my age. If I didn't drink lots of cold liquids, my mouth would get so dry I thought I would die. At summer camp growing up, my mother had to give the school infirmary a note that said "my son needs to have more water or liquids than most children". And I remember those scorching hot days, waiting with a dry palate for the snack shack to open at three pm at camp. I couldn't wait to get my ice-cold Welch's Grape Soda or Root Beer. I would suck the whole thing down in one gulp. It's as if I was still gasping for air, but drinking the water I almost drowned on instead. This event was one of the key problems causing my head issue.

I carried the baggage of this event with me for years, not knowing how it was affecting my life and making me behave. I loved water and only wanted to live on the water and be around the pool all the time, as though I was maybe trying to solve a mystery from my childhood. It caused me to be afraid of people, thinking danger was lurking at every turn. Some things in our life are so obvious—they are right there in front us, just below the surface, but we still fail to see them.

I would also like to share with you an example of an EFT release. This occurred to a video titled "Fear of Never Getting Better" on EFT Master Brad Yates' YouTube channel. If you don't know Brad, he is an exceptional EFT practitioner and I highly encourage everyone to work with him, buy all his books and tap to his wonderful YouTube tapping videos.

This EFT video helped me tremendously because it was all about clearing the fear from my energy system of being sick. When a person is ill for a long time as I was, a part of us begins to hold the fear that the condition will never leave. We are so afraid of being sick, that we are constantly fighting and rejecting it sort of. By pushing it away like that we are only causing it to manifest again and again because the fear itself is strong and the attention is always on the problem *not the solution.* Tapping to this video daily for a few weeks caused me to clear most of this fear out that kept manifesting in my life.

3

SPIRITUALITY TECHNOLOGIES

When I was ten years old in 1990, my mother, Charme Tate, had a profound mystical experience at our home in Jackson, Mississippi, that would change our whole family's lives forever.

Standing in the kitchen one day cutting a carrot, she was feeling very depressed about some of the circumstances in our family at that time. The son of a very dear friend of ours was an alcoholic and had been living with us temporarily, until my mother was forced to ask him to leave.

All of a sudden, while feeling distraught, she saw this blinding white light, had a sense of the history of everything that had ever happened and would happen. She saw waterfalls of energy rushing in front of her accompanied by a profound sense of peace. She knew that if she moved into the light, she would die, and something told her she needed to stay behind to raise me.

The week after the experience, my mother said she felt very peaceful and relaxed. I remember that week like it was yesterday because she told me about her experience and we spent one afternoon playing ball, which was an activity usually reserved for my father and me.

After that day, my mother joined the Episcopal church, began reading lots of spiritual books and deeply studied the Enneagram personality system. This eventually led to my deeper interest in Sufism, since the Enneagram theory is a Sufic model brought to America by the Russo-Armenian Sufi mystic George Ivanovich Gurdjieff (1877–1949).

It just so happens that my mother's grandfather, Wilbur Buckner, had a similar experience. While walking through the woods during his rounds as a postman in 1919, he was struck by a blinding white light and fell to the ground, dropping his mail bag. After that moment, he knew he wanted to be a preacher. He was a Baptist minister his whole life and would often attend the sick and dying. My mother tells me he could see a dying person's spirit leave their body.

Both of these experiences impacted me in a profound way, for I knew there was something more to life than the banal. God was a part of my life from the moment my mother had that experience, and the search for truth has never left me.

Since I was born the day before July 4th, it seems my whole life has centered around the theme of independence. I have an overwhelming obsession with freedom, insofar as it concerns the personal decision to choose the foods we eat, the ideas we hold, the religious paths we follow, the paper money we use and how it is manipulated, and freedom from destructive ideas and practices. Anything can become a form of slavery if you let it. The TV, a watch, music, another person, fame, anything!

A spiritual technology such as The Sufi Tradition can free us from our conditioning, Dede says. Let me now give you a very important example from my own life and how The Tradition gave me the tools to free me from some of my conditioning.

I grew up a slave to movies and lived to watch them.

During my time with Ali Dede, although I was

going through a lot of healing and inner work re-
lated to my health which did indeed occupy a lot
of time, I was so obsessed by movies that I often
neglected the more important Inner Exercises that
accelerate enlightenment. Instead, I would watch
movies every evening—and sometimes all day as
well. I neglected some very important spiritual
reading too. The TV had become my church. Not
to dismiss the cinematic arts—there are some
truly profound and wonderful movies out there—
my point is that my focus was primarily on
numbing out and being visually entertained all
the time, *not learning*. It was a way of going to sleep
in my life. I was so chronically stressed from childhood issues at the time that I wasn't ready to
wake up.

My parents loved movies more than anyone I
have ever known. The 80s and 90s of my childhood were eras of great John Hughes movies, and
others too. Films like *What About Bob?* (1991), *Home
Alone* (1990) and *The Great Outdoors* (1988) were on
every week.

For my family, going to the movies was the best
thing to do on a weekend. As a result, I became
very attached to the cinematic arts. As a child, I
binge-watched films from A to Z. Perceiving this
desire in me, for years, my guide only allowed me

to watch movies and TV (except for the nightly news) on Friday and Saturday nights. At first this exercise was hard to endure, almost excruciating, but I let go of my desire. And when I was finally permitted to watch what I wanted to at the time I wanted, I no longer cared about it. My love for reading was also renewed, and I found even more value in books than before. These days, I am a voracious reader, and love to learn through reading. The recipe to cure my obsession with films was to give up watching them obsessively for some time until I was free of the desire.

Another thing that has broken down much of my conditioning is being criticized in a healthy way by my spirit guide. At first I was so angry, almost furious at being criticized, but after a while, I learned how to be neutral to it. This neutrality transferred over to other areas of my life as well. I found if someone attacked me verbally for my beliefs or something I said, I felt stronger because I could detach from it. I also found myself eating half of a delicious plate of food and being able to stop, instead of lusting after the rest of it as I once had. I once felt a sort of strange compulsion inherent in my nature, possibly conditioned from childhood or due to my enneagram number 8 type (a personality type which is obsessed with over-stimulation and therefore tends to abuse stuff), to consume things like a blaze of wildfire, scorching anything I came into contact with.

That compulsion had been totally beyond my control, causing me to abuse certain things such as tobacco, tea, alcohol, coffee, greasy food, sugar, even shopping. Now I could be in the moment, detach from the compulsion, and choose to refrain from these things, even if just for one day. Doing this repeatedly created a certain serene feeling of well-being and calm, and in my inner self, I felt like I had finally achieved some state of happiness.

Fasting has also been most beneficial for detaching my dependence on bad food. I consider intermittent fasting, or not eating for a whole sixteen-hour period and then eating for the other eight hours in a day to be a truly useful practice. After fasting for a while, you learn to appreciate the subtle taste and flavor of foods. You also realize you can function without food at all temporarily and even feel lighter and clearer with less food in your system. I am not advising anyone to fast for prolonged time periods without the guidance of a specialist, however.

Along my journey, I was once lusting after a tasty piece of meat, and my second Sufi Teacher, which I will keep anonymous for now, psychically removed all the energy from my body and being. The world felt completely dead and empty. Nothing had any life and I had no hunger at all, and when I did eat, the food tasted like cardboard. I asked her what she had done, and she replied that she was showing me that it was only God that sustained me—*not food*. What gave me energy in food was Reality. After a few hours, she returned the energy.

These things aside, the single most important conditioning lesson I have learned in The Sufi Tradition is how to be still and be one with the ever-present moment of the now. How to refrain from doing something else just to be keeping busy. How to sit for long periods of time and do nothing and be okay with that. Growing up in the West, I was obsessed with doing something all the time just to be busy. But we do not need to fill every moment with noise pollution and visual stimulation from TV, phones, music, and computers. We need to learn how to breathe, be in nature and focus on what really matters—our inner selves.

Do view Ali Dede's You Tube channel for free Inner Exercises from The Great Sufi Tradition: https://bit.ly/2RVToFW

Teaching stories like those found in The Great Tradition of the Sufis also accelerate inner growth.

You can access thousands of these in the books of Sufi Teacher, Idries Shah (1924–1996), available for purchase on the Idries Shah Foundation's website and online. There are many others for free on ISF's YouTube channel (see resources at the end of this book for links). Some of these stories are about the wise fool, Nasrudin. Others are more elaborate teaching stories. All of them contain many levels of understanding: on the surface, they may make us laugh or entertain us, while at a deeper level, they enable us to transform by revealing things about life and ourselves that we might not have previously perceived. In this way, they are blueprints for the mind.

Back in 2003 when I was searching for a Sufi Teacher, I wrote to the Nobel Prize-winning British author of countless books, Doris Lessing, for help. I knew she had been a student of Idries Shah's and thought she could point me in the right direction. At the time, I told her that I had read almost all of Shah's books (and there are dozens) and hoped I was ready to take the next step and find a Sufi Teacher.

She typed me a letter back shortly after, stating that my desire for a teacher was alarming to her and that I should read all of Shah's books again— that there was so much there to learn. I share this with you because these books are spiritually instructive and preparatory on their own. Shortly after, I came to realize that Idries Shah had been my first teacher inadvertently through his books.

ANOTHER TECHNOLOGY that has been beneficial to me was developed by Dr. Frank Kinslow, a Sarasota-based Florida chiropractic physician. Quantum Entrainment, which Dede asserts is similar in many ways to the technology of The Tradition, provides inner exercises such as The Gate Technique, Sensation Exercise and EuFeeling, that are designed to develop the human's inner being, placing him or her in a state of peace and wellbeing.

From my personal experience of working with Quantum Entrainment and reading most of Kinslow's books, I can attest that they have profoundly positive benefits. When practicing EuFeeling, the student is asked to notice the space between thoughts, then to observe what EuFeeling they feel. This observation of the space between thoughts stops the ego, creating a connection to the inner self, which is joined with the higher frequencies of Love, Grace, Peace, Thankfulness and Joy. This expands as one gets better with time. Ultimately, we already are spiritual beings, although we may not be aware of it. Quantum Entrainment puts us back there again in an instant! (See the resources section in the back of this book for more information on QE.)

4

QUANTUM TOOLS

In this chapter, I am going to discuss a few other therapies and tools I feel are worthy of mention and are more quantum in their application.

The first is coffee.

If you have read my other books, then you will know that my favorite substance in the world to harp on about is coffee. First of all, I absolutely love it. Unfortunately, I also am a nervous wreck after just one cup. I can't even tolerate one half cup of this specially prepared coffee I will tell you about now, but maybe if you do okay with coffee and you are going to drink it anyway, this might be useful for you to know about.

Recently, Dede informed me that coffee, when

properly prepared, can have a truly beneficial effect on the mind. This revolution, called the Fourth Wave, is well documented in the book *The Fourth Wave: A Fresh Roasting Revolution* by Asher Yaron.

Yaron, who lives in Bali, describes how when coffee was first used in Sufi monasteries, it was roasted, immediately ground, brewed and consumed right away. This process, known as "fresh roasting," produces not only the best tasting coffee, but also coffee with a spiritual effect on the mind and the body. It's roughly equivalent to the difference between cooked vegetable and fruit juices and raw, fresh juices. When coffee is prepared in this way, all the antioxidants are still intact.

Dede states that the only problem with consuming any coffee, even fresh-roasted and brewed, is a magnesium deficiency. Supplementing with 500 mgs of magnesium a day remedies it.

The next therapy is hydrogen.

Dede maintains that one of the most important health developments of this century is a water generator that makes molecular hydrogen. The one he recommended for me, and the only one I use, is LevelWayUp: Glass Hydrogen Water Bottle Generator, available online (see links on my author webpage here: https://www.duketateauthor.com/gifts). This glass hydrogen generator is affordable, costing a mere $90, and releases molecular hydrogen into the water in about three minutes after starting the machine. The water must be consumed directly after the generator finishes, as the hydrogen dissipates quickly after it is made.

Molecular hydrogen (symbol H and atomic weight of 1.008 on the periodic table) is the most powerful antioxidant in the world. It is a thousand times more powerful than Vitamin C and is also the smallest element in existence (almost 100 times smaller than Vitamin C), allowing it to penetrate our cells where it can eliminate free radicals at their source. Unlike other antioxidants, hydrogen can distinguish between good and bad free radicals, and only target the bad ones, which are converted into water when it binds with them. (Primo H2, n.d.) Over 350 scientific studies have been conducted on the benefits of hydrogen. You can learn more in the resources section of this book.

When I am traveling, I take Primo H2 capsules so I don't have to bring the water generator with me.

. . .

DEALING with chronic illness of any kind is truly a challenge whether a person is spiritual or not. I know—I had a whole range of seemingly incurable illnesses from the age of nineteen until about age twenty-nine. Ten years of suffering.

When I wrote the first book in this series, *Returning to Freedom: Breaking the Bonds of Chemical Sensitivity and Lyme Disease*, I was disappointed in how little I had to say on the subject in terms of page numbers. I had always imagined myself writing some grand 500-page book about my journey, but the truth was, many days during that ten-year time period were quite boring, almost excruciating.

Who wants to read detailed accounts of me sitting around watching movies all day laid up in bed? I can tell you I saw almost every movie ever made, twice! That's what you do when you can't work, date or go to college. If you have a chronic illness, the most important thing is to keep faith, stay strong and remember—people who are successful in things have that one single trait in common: stickability. Don't ever lose it.

I thought my head numbness would never get better. But it did. I thought my erectile dysfunction would never get better. But it did. What if I had given up half-way through trying to rid myself of both conditions? I wouldn't have anything to tell you now, would I? I likely wouldn't be married either, due to the ED.

During the ten years I was ill, I went through every range of human emotion: feeling sorry for myself, being angry at the world and myself, being angry at my parents... and none of that helped. What helped was doing things in a calm, peaceful and extremely careful way, with the guidance of my Teachers.

When taking any new medicinal such as the hydrogen water, it is crucial to start at a snail's pace. By that I mean start with one ounce of the hydrogen water on the first day. Do that for a few days, then go to three ounces. If you handle that well, go on to four and so on. If you don't do well with it, do not force taking it. Not everything is good for every person. You might be better with zero nutrients and hydrogen. See what works best for your body and never force anything. You have to tune into what your body needs at any given moment.

When I had chronic candidiasis, which caused my multiple chemical sensitivities, I was so delicate that just one single drop of Cellfood (a stabilized oxygen and mineral supplement) in water caused me to have diarrhea. Good thing I didn't overdo it at first! Of course, now I can take it eight drops 3 times a day no problem. You see how it works?

Sometimes, I was so desperate to feel better that I forced therapies and treatments, only to suffer feeling worse from it. Never <u>force</u> anything. I can't say this enough. The body is organic. It takes time to adjust to things. And everyone's body is different. People don't need all the same things.

IN THE SECOND book in this Big Journey series: *Gifts from a Guide: Life Hacks from a Spiritual Teacher*, I mention that certain places—cities, sacred churches, shrines, mausoleums—have a certain spiritual energy (*baraka*) to them. It can be most beneficial to spend some time in these places for health and inner work. When I arrived in Tokyo, for example, I was ill as I had been before I left. After getting to my hotel and waking up the next day, I was miraculously 100% well, even though I had not taken or done anything special to aid in my recovery. The place was that beneficial for my health.

· · ·

Now, I will also review the Quantum Pulse machine I speak about in *Gifts from a Guide: Life Hacks from a Spiritual Teacher*. If you read that book, you can skip over this section if you like.

When I was very ill with Lyme Disease and Multiple Chemical Sensitivities, one machine—the Vibe Machine—helped me tremendously. My family owned two of these devices, one for myself and the other for my parents. Developed by Gene Koonce, a Colorado electronic repair store-owner and former army missile technician who worked on inventions in his spare time, the Vibe Machine (now going by the name Quantum Pulse) is a triumphant breakthrough in the field of energy medicine. The machine uses spectrum tubes that contain noble gases (that fall between the infrared and ultraviolet spectrum range) and a multi-wave oscillator, the combination producing bio-photonic light in an electromagnetic field within a radius of six to eight feet around the machine.

The first time Dede recommended I try the Vibe Machine, I was in Half Moon Bay, California, just south of San Francisco. My mother, Charme Tate, was visiting a chiropractor's house right on the ocean. Half Moon Bay is a truly picturesque town that crests along the Pacific. Home to "Maverick", one of the largest and most brutal waves that surfers love to ride, it's a hip town with a true California vibe where people still ride horses on the beach. Dr. Joe, the humble, middle-aged lady who owned the Vibe Machine, had the clearest light blue eyes I had ever seen (other than those of the raw food guru, Aajonus Vonderplanitz). She surfed every day, and had a radiant glow to her skin. She informed us she used the machine for ten minutes a day, every day. We sat close to it in a dark room for three minutes while the machine made a loud noise and the glass tubes lit up as the various gases flowed through them. The physical effect was immediate: the sensation of increased energy in the body, peace, and calm. While the Vibe Machine alone didn't cure me of Lyme Disease or Chemical Sensitivities, it did help me to feel much better and increase my energy. I wasn't able to use it consistently due to not being able to transport the large apparatus when moving a lot, so we may never know the effect it could have had if used continuously for a long period.

5

QUESTIONS & ANSWERS
WITH DUKE

What do you consider to be the most important therapy you have ever tried?

The best physical therapy I have ever tried is stabilized oxygen such as Cellfood. Also hydrogen water for detoxification. Vitamin D has been very important for my immune health, so I take 10,000 IUs of it every day. And EFT and Dr. Alex Loyd's *The Healing Codes* have been so useful for me in many different ways to help let go of my past perturbations. I would say these five therapies have changed my life the most.

Comment on detox. How do you get through it?

Well, it's very important when doing any therapy, including emotional therapy such as *The Healing Codes* and EFT, to go slowly and not overdo anything. <u>Never force</u> anything. Even emotional therapies can cause detox in the form of headaches, body aches and even diarrhea. I have never had EFT or TFT cause a detox, but I have had these special healing codes cause it. So, it's always important to never overdo. Go slowly, work up, if you get to a point where you are having a detox from a healing code, take a day or days off and rest. One time with *the Healing Codes*, while working through some issues, I had some depression come up—something which I never experience, so I used Dr. Loyd's love code from his book *The Love Codes* which was very, very effective at healing the sadness quickly. Working with these codes is like peeling an onion. When you remove one thing, something else can bubble up to the surface.

Whenever I have had detox, eating white rice seems to really help do away with it. Also drinking lots of spring water.

How long were you ill?

Well, I was ill a long time. Many, many years. I would say about ten years of acute illness, but I have dealt with various symptoms for probably fifteen years. Getting well again from serious chronic illness can require perseverance, stickability and faith. Never give up. Always remember there is an answer out there—there is a solution. Different things work for different people and different conditions. Stay strong and never lose faith.

How can emotional problems lead to physical problems?

Bestselling author Dr. Bruce Lipton, Phd of Stanford University talks about how memories are stored at a cellular level, affecting every cell in our bodies, and in that way, emotional problems can develop into physical problems. That doesn't mean that they aren't physical problems, it just means that stress is what led to the problem at some level. Stress reduces our immune system, causing all sorts of issues. Dede says the body needs a state of peace for the immune system to function properly. It will always be worth addressing any condition from multiple avenues. If you have a physical condition, trying to eliminate the emotional problems is wise, but trying to treat the physical condition is wise too because at the point you have it, it *is* a physical condition. There is nothing wrong with trying to work on the physical aspect as well. However, if underlying emotional problems are not treated, the physical problem may go away and return later on.

Talk about having a spiritual path. How can a spiritual path undo conditioning?

The goal of all spiritual paths is to undo all conditioning at some level, although it may be a slow process. There are many different ways the path does that. Mainly it is retraining your body, mind and spirit to act in different ways. I discuss in the book various things my Teachers did with me to undo my conditioning. Positive criticism can undo conditioning. That is very different from unconscious criticism because the guide knows the student's faults and how to correct them, whereas unconscious criticism is often just to ridicule someone without knowing whether it will be helpful or hurtful. The critic may even feel pleasure in this, which a teaching master never would.

Part of my path has involved abstinence. Conscious suffering undoes conditioning. Suffering is different for different people. Some people are not attached at all to coffee, cigarettes, alcohol and bad food. For other people like myself, we are very attached to those things, so they have to be eliminated.

In any case, everybody alive today has to give up those things eventually—when we leave this place. Everybody gives them up when they die. Taking those steps before you actually die is a way of preparing yourself physically, mentally and emotionally to sustain on God's energy alone and not all these other things. However, I surmise that when a person does finally reach enlightenment those things have so little effect, they can even ground a person in the world. That's why you will see all these Sufi masters sitting around smoking cigars and drinking coffee. They have totally eclipsed it and it doesn't have any effect on them.

But for me, giving up things on my particular path has allowed me to undo some of my conditioning, and living without them has contributed to a more spiritual life for me.

It's about being what the Sufis call Master of the Option. If a person has a compulsion to do something, they are not Master of the Option. They don't have a free choice to do it or not do it.

That ties back into conditioning in that we are all trained to desire things for emotional reasons. We do it to ease our pain and suffering, or at least we think we do. However, the thing itself becomes another form of suffering that we take on.

I was extremely addicted to coffee. I thought I needed it to write and be happy. I was totally wrong about it, but I couldn't see it. It made me a nervous wreck—a complete basket case. My writing was unfocused and stressful. I finally gave it up for good and am so happy to be free of it.

Discuss taking clues from dreams.

When I first got ill in 1999, I began having very vivid dreams. And I have continued to have dreams for as long as I was tuned into them. I have even had dreams that were prescient where I dreamed something and the next day, it actually happened. One time, while living in Los Angeles, I dreamed that a friend I was supposed to meet the next day would call and say he couldn't make it. And sure enough, he called the next day and said he couldn't come. Another time, I lost my wallet, and dreamed about its location.

I used to have a Jungian depth therapist. When interpreting my dreams, sometimes he was on and

sometimes he was off . Overall, he was very helpful. The most important thing is to go with what is
obvious in the dream for you. Let it sink in. Don't
try to over-analyze it if you don't know what it
means. Just live with it and over time it will reveal
itself to you. Dreams can be warnings—they can
be foresights. My senior year in high school, I was
experimenting with drugs and had a very dis-
turbing dream where I was on a staircase at my
boarding school with a guy who was selling drugs
at the school. The dream had no color to it—it was
burned out. We were doing a deal for some mari-
juana in the stairwell and then the dream ended.
That dream was a warning for me, for I had only
really experimented with drugs my senior year in
high school. The dream scared me. It felt like
death to me. It felt cold. And I decided to stop
what I was doing. Fortunately, I got sick with Lyme
Disease and was forced to stop everything. It was a
blessing in disguise.

The most important thing with dreams is
never to think that a certain thing always means
the same thing in every dream. That a snake always means deceit, for instance. Each dream is
unique for the dreamer at any given time in their
life. For instance, in one dream a snake could
mean deceit and in another one, it could represent

rebirth, because a snake sheds its skin. I don't care too much for dream interpretation books unless they teach you about symbolism in general, but don't ever apply those symbols without knowledge or perception. The dream is a living thing, in the way that a Sufi story is. It has an essence, something it is trying to convey to you. Slowly over time it will reveal itself to you.

What is the best approach to diet?

While I am not a doctor or a nutritionist, my philosophy about diet is to keep it simple and eat less when it comes to food. The Zone Diet is the best framework out there in my opinion. It involves eating protein, carbohydrates and fats in exact proportions calculated by Dr. Barry Sears. The easiest way to estimate it is to fill ¾ of your plate up with fruits and vegetables and ¼ of it with a low fat meat, then add a dash of healthy fat like olive oil or coconut oil to it. Sometimes it is very hard to follow, especially when traveling, because it requires eating foods in precise portions.

Drinking lots of hydrogen-rich structured spring water, taking in good quality food from unpolluted sources, getting enough raw fruits and vegetables and also eating less meat than we eat in

America are all very good dietary tips. Living in Thailand now, I really believe in the power of chilis and cayenne. I feel my best after I eat a spicy dish with lots of chili. It increases circulation and opens the sinuses. Also no one in Thailand eats dairy and they are all very slim. Staying alkaline at a cellular level is very important as well.[1] I would advise the following as general rules of thumb:

- drink lots of real structured water
- never eat white sugar
- never drink hard liquor (use red wine instead)
- minimize dairy
- eat gluten free
- minimize eggs
- eat lots of raw fruits and veggies

Discuss EFT and the healing codes.

I started out tapping with TFT and EFT in 2005. I have used them for a lot of issues ever since and had great success with them. I believe that Dr. Alex Loyd's *Healing Codes* achieve similar results to EFT or TFT, although often in a much shorter timeframe for certain things. I think there is a time and place for both. Some issues like addictions may respond much better to tapping and others like health ails to the codes.

I will give you another example of how these codes work from my personal use of them. When I was fourteen, I was going to a high school party. We were not invited, and right as we approached it this big, muscle-bound dude from another school pushed me really hard while telling me to get lost. Cocky and stupid, I made the mistake of pushing him back. And right away, he knocked me out with a strong right forearm, sending me slamming onto the ground and breaking my glasses.

Being fourteen, the effect that punch had on me was to make me want to be strong throughout my whole life. I didn't want to be pushed around like that ever again. I was a lanky fourteen-year-old who failed miserably at every jock sport he played due to being scrawny and weak.

See, there was a lie written on that memory of being punched, because being muscular doesn't necessarily protect you from harm, nor does it make you good at sports. We have conditioned beliefs that aren't true, written on our hearts, and they affect everything we do. It would be better to take a martial arts class to learn protection than lift weights. There are people who are very muscular who can't fight well. But in my mind I believed that if I were strong, I would be protected, and perhaps I also thought I would be healthy. There is nothing wrong with exercising and being strong if a person does it for the right reasons. Having muscle increases metabolism to burn fat, looks better, and exercising releases endorphins, which makes us feel good. But I was hitting the gym my whole life for a different reason – to win a fight. Practicing the Healing Codes clarified the true meaning of the event at the party, and freed me from my misplaced reaction to it.

Talk about peace.

The single most important element of my spiritual path has been peace. Because I was an anxious child, I experienced a lot of stress and tension. Just learning to be still and not drowning in social media, information and television has been so important for me. Being able to sit and be one with everything that is around me without having to be inundated with noise all the time is so healthy. It is also important to learn to be at peace whilst engaged in tasks. I think you learn to hold peace the more familiar you become with it. Cutting coffee is so important for me in maintaining a state of peace. Some people are so normal on caffeine, but others like myself are a nervous wreck.

How have you cured your anxiety disorder?

Well, recently in 2020, Ali Dede sent me a remarkable book titled *Breath* by James Nestor. In it he discusses the science of breath and how incredibly important it is to breathe through the nose. Mouth breathing causes hyperventilation which causes anxiety and panic. I discuss the benefits of nose-breathing in Book 2 of this series.[2]

I must attest that breathing through the nose throughout the whole day has helped me almost completely eliminate my anxiety disorder, which was so severe for many years. Nestor covers the Dutch extreme athlete The Iceman or Wim Hof's breathing technique The Wim Hof Method, which involves breathing deeply in a fast method without pause, then holding one's breath and cycling back to the fast breathwork and doing this for many rounds. This breathwork is roughly similar to the Tibetan Buddhist monk's method of tummo breathing. Wim's Method has been scientifically proven to boost the immune system.

Other tools like Inner Work given to me by Dede, EFT and TFT and the Healing Codes have also helped with my anxiety. Eliminating coffee may be the single most important thing anyone can do to stop anxiety because coffee depletes magnesium (the relaxation mineral) and contains a tremendous amount of caffeine, especially Robusta brands, which should be avoided completely.

Where are you now?

I am in Thailand right now. Still not a Sufi yet, but I want to be. One thing I am learning from being here is that Thai people have a natural sort of Zen to them. All Thai men are required to be Buddhist monks at a certain age. And they all learn how to get over things without making a big fuss about it.

Constructively talking about a problem in a way to bring solutions to the surface can be very useful, but juicing about problems with no end in sight because we get some bizarre thrill from it is counterproductive. We can all learn from Thai people this simple trait of how to avoid the quagmire of complaining.

QUANTUM WORLD

Today, we live in unprecedented times. With the internet and smart phones, everyone has access to knowledge at the push of a button. Almost anyone anywhere can send a message or video out in a matter of seconds to the whole world if they like.

It is an age of miracles.

Quantum computing is on the rise, which should accelerate the introduction of Artificial Intelligence (AI robots) into our daily lives and advance the role that holographic images will take in movies and technology.

Some online stores are beginning to use drones to deliver packages in one day. Imagine that!

The quantum financial system is taking over as well, where the slow, antiquated Swift method of sending money will collapse, and money will be transferred instantly over various cryptocurrencies.

Central bank digital currencies (CBDCs) are starting to appear on the horizon, like the Chinese digital Yuan, which will allow people to pay for things with a smartphone app as though it were cash.

3D printers can now print body parts, houses and metal of any shape instantly.

In this new world, everything is happening so fast, it's hard to keep up. It's amazing, wonderful and highly stressful at the same time. Reference the therapies I share in this book with grace and kindness. Some were designed to set us at ease. Find a real health pro like Dede to help you if you are in need.

I wish you and your loved ones health and well-being in these times. Stay safe!

RESOURCES

Ali Dede's website: www.thesufitradition.com

Dede's YouTube channel: https://rb.gy/gzerkv

Idries Shah Foundation: https://idriesshahfounda
tion.org

Kinslow System: https://kinslowsystem.com/home

Dr. Alex Loyd's Healing Codes: https://www.
dralexanderloyd.com

NOTES

2. Quantum Health

1. See page 9-10 in *Gifts from a Guide: Life Hacks from a Spiritual Teacher*
2. See page 2 in *Gifts from a Guide: Life Hacks from a Spiritual Teacher*

5. Questions & Answers with Duke

1. See page 21 in *Gifts from a Guide*
2. See page 15 in *Gifts from a Guide*

ABOUT THE AUTHOR

Duke Tate was born in Mississippi where he grew up surrounded by an age-old tradition of story-telling common to the deep South. He currently lives in Southeast Florida where he enjoys fishing, surfing, cooking Asian food and reading.

You can view his YouTube channel here and his author website here.

a amazon.com/Duke-Tate

g goodreads.com/9784192.Duke_Tate

f facebook.com/duketateauthor

X x.com/duke_tate

ALSO BY DUKE TATE

Bugspray

Short Reads

The Biscuit and *The Burger Flip Kid*

Santa's Magic Bag and *Bottom of the Ninth*

Sasquatch's Cereal and *Eccentrification*

The Venus 2.0

The Wordsmith

With Ken Tate

Only the Painting Knows the Whole Story and *The Pink Lady*

The Alchemy of Architecture: Memories and Insights from Ken Tate

With Wiphawan Tate

Musings of an American Redhead in Thailand

The Pearlmakers

Book 1: The Hunt for La Gracia

Book 2: The Dollarhide Mystery

Book 3: Gold is in the Air

The Pearlmakers: The Trilogy

Big John Series

Big John and the Fortune Teller

Big John and the Island of Bones

Big John and the Hitcher

Big John's Hair-Raising Misadventures: The Trilogy

My Big Journey

Returning to Freedom: Breaking the Bonds of Chemical Sensitivities and Lyme Disease

Gifts from A Guide: Life Hacks from A Spiritual Teacher

Translations

Gifts from A Guide: Life Hacks from A Spiritual Teacher - Spanish edition

Gifts from A Guide: Life Hacks from A Spiritual Teacher - Dutch edition

Big John and the Fortune Teller - Thai edition

Quantum Living: A Life Full of Miracles - Spanish edition

Upcoming Titles

The Cobbler

Thrive

Jericho Walker: Mississippi Lizard Hunter and Other Short Stories

M